Will It Be A Bad Night In Itaewon Series By Jason Changkyu Kim

Purister Publishing and Outsourcing.

"Will It Be A Bad Night in Itaewon? A Letter Penned from the Heart."

A Leveled Reader Novel by Jason Changkyu Kim

Description: The impetuous Haebin Can't wait to grow up and go out with her friends. Will her father let her ruin her life? We're see about that.

Drama.

"Haebin, your going out with the girls tonight to Itaewon?" Said Father

"Dad, I went to a girls school my whole life. Elementary, Middle, High School and even my university was all girls. I just want to meet a nice stallion and run off to the sunset!" Said Haebin as she was putting on makeup.

"Father, its going to be fine. I met Josh, he's with the United States Army, he's stationed in Itaewon. We're pen pals through Korea University's "Practice English" Program." Said Haebin

"He's nice, I checked him out online, hes my age. And he went to

college at Cornell. He's Ivy League. I was wondering what that meant.

Its a very high level school. Hes an artist! A graphic arts major!" Said

Haebin with so much enthusiasm.

Her Father just sat in the corner with a bag of potato chips. "Honey

South Korea has potato chips too. See? Honey I don't feel right about

it. See? It's American, Lays."

"Dad this is more than about potato chips. Why work? I went to

college to become a house wife." Said Haebin

"He's rich, he has a job, he's so sophisticated. Maybe two years older

than me? Maybe? You met him, Josh is

fantastic!" Said Haebin

Her Father just laughed, hiding it. "I like it,

Potato Chips! I like him,

kind of. But honey Itaewon is not for a young

girl. It's all bars and

clubs. Please stay with me tonight. We're doing

scrap booking and

checkbooks again. Don't make me stalk you!."

He chuckled hiding the

tears.

"Daddy, Josh is from Arkansas, he joined the

Marines right after

college. He was in the Officer Training Corps! I studied English my

whole life and there's no where to use it." Said Haebin

Dad just got a sparkle in his eyes "Honey the Marines and the Army

are two different things. Just because Josh is pretty now does not

mean he'll be pretty in 30 years. Men don't age like my beautiful

daughter here."

"Come on dad, I don't blame you for mom leaving. See? She'll be

back with groceries later tonight." Said Haebin

"We got all our relatives, your not leaving alone tonight. We called a

hunsan clan meeting. Your aunts, uncles, and your friends parents are

bunching up tonight. If I see too much drinking. We're going home.

Got it?" Said her father sternly.

Haebin began to pout "Dad that's so not cool. It's just a couple drinks

with some Navy guys too."

Haebin went on "Dad I'm going to America to study at Evergreen

University in Washington. Your professor friend set it up, remember?

This is the last chance to get married before I'm
an American girl now.
I can't, can't, can't pass up the last chance to
party before I have to
spend all night studying again. Evergreen has
the best Master's in
Teaching program in the world! I can't, can't,
can't give up this chance.
I'm meeting Josh. We even talked about the
future, he's going back to
school with me!"
Her father just shrugged. Almost derisively
started laughing in the
corner of the room with his legs crossed and an
open bag of potato

chips. "Honey if hes stationed in Korea, he has an enlistment date, do

you know what I'm saying? It's not a normal job, he can't just pack up

and leave when he feels like it. Every boy in Korea served in the army.

I'm not racist, you can't date a nice Korean boy instead?"

Haebin got impatient and started stamping her feet "Papa, it's fine, the

professor and the school thinks its fine too! He's great!"

Her father got impatient back. "So what's the plan tonight?"

Haebin said "Josh planned everything, we're going night clubbing at a

hip hop club called Noise Basement, we're eating at Mcdonald's, and

some coffee at Starbucks, you know how much I adore coffee, and

buying some tea in Seoul."

"Honey we only moved to Seoul a few years ago. Going to

Itaewon is 2 hours away. I don't trust Josh. Honey no! I finally said it,

it's a no! You can't hang out with Josh." Her Father started yelling

"Its an American joke, you propose in McDonalds with french fries and onion rings. I don't like you hanging out at bars and night clubs, your

only 22. Please don't ruin your life. Stay here with me forever." Without

hesitating, he ran to his room. Pulled out a baseball bat, American and

barred the door with a couch and sat around with a half eaten bag of

potato chips. And that's that! He thought!

The Next Morning

Haebin thought to herself, My gosh my dad ruined my night. All night I

cried about how am I going to tell my friends I had to ditch them on our night on the town. I went downstairs expecting to find my sweet old father on the couch sprawled out in his underwear. But, he was gone as usual around 3:00 AM in the morning. For years I thought my father was a truck driver. A humble position, around middle school I found out dad has his own street food truck. A used blue Daewoo 1997 pick up truck. He used to be a beer delivery driver with his old Dayton Hand Truck until he found out selling food $2.00 at a time was worth it.

I wondered all day if it was worth it, $2.00 is $2.00. I found out he also

owns a drop shipping website. He explained it to me in when I was in university.

"It might not seem right. But I use something called 'Ghost

Shoppers',Your aunt visits costco in Jangam on Tuesdays with her

family and I visit on Fridays with your mother. And your uncle visits on

Wednesday's with his wife. Our website www.costlove.com limits

orders to 200 customers a week. And we buy extra food, I have to buy food anyway for my street food stall. We like to call ourselves "Your

Personal Shoppers. Give me a list and I'll send everything to you in a

Styrofoam box filled with ice." My Father explained carefully.

"But Father, that's not right. What if you get caught? A store is a store,

you have inventory and you have a place to sell it." Said Haebin

"I know sweetheart" Said her father earnestly.

"But the money was too

good to be true. I list everything on online shopping websites in South Korea and they found out and fined me. I paid 7.2 million won, almost $7,200 United

States Dollars. It's not illegal and the money is good. And I really enjoy

having a store without the risk of buying too much inventory that will

not sell later. I feel good but nervous every time I go to the store on

Fridays."

Haebin sighed and did not say anything. Then paused and asked

pointedly "So you buy only when you get an order? Like 14 more

pieces of American Deli ham?"

Her father said "Pretty much yeah. With my regular customers, we have our membership program so I can figure out here and there how much I need so I can buy a little more. And you know I make sandwiches so I can always freeze the extra ham and cheese."

"I really did not enjoy being a beer delivery drive Haebin. I felt like I stole people's lives away" Said her father, "Sandwiches does not seem like big money. But, customers usually buy three to four at a time. During subway rush in Itaewon… And I

am sorry about Joshua."

He paused for awhile then smiled and petted her

hair. I really love

talking to my daughter he thought.

"Any exit at Itaewon station

during the early morning rush hour around 6:00

AM the subway

opens. All those drunk kids that went night

clubbing and drinking got

locked out. I know Itaewon honey. The first bar

closes around 2:00 in

the morning and the night clubs close around

1:00 AM. The subway

already closed at 12:30; around midnight. All those kids are tired, they

spent all their money, and they are looking for something cheap to eat.

You really ought to be careful there honey.

Itaewon is not for little kids.

The United States Army base closes their gates at 8:30 PM, all those

army boys are back in their apartments by 9:00 at night I think. And

they don't get fired or yelled at. I don't think Joshua was army; number

1 and number 2 if he was. I don't know if his Captain will let him drink

all night and come back to work tomorrow.
Honey please promise me,
you stay my little chicken hen forever? Pretty
please?"
Her father went on fanatically "These United
States Army guys drink
all night and hit on girls left and right. Its not
fair, as a father I feel so
much heartbreak on my drunk patrol. I go with
your uncle who's a taxi
driver and we check for people who drank too
much. Itaewon is too
dangerous for Korean girls. I know it seems like
~Manhattan." He said

laughing and twirling his shoulders back and forth. "But New York City

is not a place for little girls. Trust me Itaewon is dangerous, all those

men are bad and they are only looking for one thing! They're not

looking to get married."

"I was talking to your uncle. We were talking about the days as beer

delivery salesmen. I told the bartenders and night club owners in

Itaewon that tonic water and American Seltzer water were good for

alcoholics in helping them quit. Do you know what they did with it?

They just turned them into Manhattan Iced Tea Cocktails. It's

sweetened Iced Tea with rum and an sweet

beverage. That's not a drink for

my child!" Her father almost started ranting

"This is the only place in Seoul that American

party drinks like

Jello-shots, you can actually buy. A jello shot is

vodka mixed with

American Jello snack desert candy. It's not fair

how dangerous this

place is Haebin" Yelled her father

"Dad it just sounds like good natured-fun. So

what if I threw up?"

Haebin was annoyed about another lecture. She thought to herself.

It's either a night with the girls or more weeks of English Hagwon

private academies.

"Dad stop! Hagwon is only important to be a house wife. I have to be a

trophy wife. I play piano, I speak English, I have a teaching degree.

Etc. Etc. Etc." Haebin shouted, annoyed now at all the nail biting rules.

"Haebin, Hagwon is why you went to Korea University.

You always wanted to go to an Ivy League.

Korea University is it!" Her

father said carefully slotting his voice to go a decibel lower.

"Haebin, sweetheart let's stop arguing. I picked up your favorite. Don't think about money. Sausages from that glamor place in Itaewon. They are one of my partners with that website you use all the time. I also got prosciutto, we're going to make sandwiches." Her father chided her to calm down.

"Dad seriously your sandwiches are good but this isn't a job." Haebin said worriedly

"Honey that's not how you talk to your father. When I was young,

South Korea was very poor. I saw so many young girls ruin their lives

to run off with American boys, soldiers and they never came home to

see their mother and father pass away. Its so sad. I make very

delicious sandwiches with egg, ketchup, mayonnaise, coleslaw, and

ham, and cheese. $2.00 is not asking much from people and I get to

share my dreams of my youth with them. Its a very fair price." He said

with such a gentle smile.

Haebin just got teary eyed and said "Dad seriously I'm sorry. Hana broke things off with Gregory and Joshua has been texting me 'What's wrong', I promise I'll just ignore him and it's over now. Okay dad?"

"Yes Haebin, Please, I'm begging you please. No more Joshua. No more of this or that. Your going to Evergreen in the Spring to attend your Master's Degree. You cannot date until you are a teacher in Seoul." Her father said mournfully.

"Haebin Honey, your uncle in Boston loves you dearly. If you go to hagwon more and study better you can stay with

our family in Boston,

he sent us another George Foreman Grill. I got

another 110 Watt to

220 Watt power converter from Yongsan

Electronics market. That

United States Army base is so ugly. Yongsan all

the way to Itaewon is

one big piece of tank property. It's not fair

honey, they've got to leave.

Anyway the George Foreman grill will cook

you a nice sausage

prosciutto sandwich tonight. And we will sing

and praise tonight at the

karaoke bar. Okay? I promise."

“Will It Be Another Bad Night in Itaewon, A Letter From the Heart.”

A

Leveled Reader Novel by Jason Changkyu Kim

Description: The impetuous Haebin Can't wait to grow up and go out

with her friends. Will her father let her ruin her life? Drama.

At the Karaoke Bar. Haebin met Syukin, her best friend since middle

school. And her Japanese cousin, Miata. Father never approved of my

friends, who always called me "Sheltered"

"I know Miata. Do you have money tonight? If not my father will pay, we are singing a Korean Classic "Men are Ships, Women are Ports by Sim Soo Bong." Said Haebin

"Fine, I have a little money." Said Miata, "We will sing Korean classics as long as you promise me I can share Japan with you with "Mariya Taekuchi's Plastic Love, it was in my favorite Japanese cartoon, Finding Techni Muyo. It's not that much of a classic. I think?"

"Syukin, you have to tell Miata that Korea and Japan are old friends now." Come lets sing. Said her father.

Later that Night... Haebin was talking to her

father to learn the secrets

of being a street food merchant. People do care

her father said. They

care a lot and stores in a city are the price of a

house. Haebin Honey,

her father thought I had to do right to your

mother and my customers

and I just could not afford to buy a store.

Okay Haebin you have to learn that Koreans

were raised in an

environment of fear because of north korea. If

you want to sell chicken

like your father and uncle

"Dad Why would I sell chicken?"

"I'm just saying" said her father quickly

"You have to memorize the gossip channels and the official news. This

is how we as a society talk to our merchants with dietary

recommendations from the central government on what to do?"

Haebin started to get serious. "I don't get it."

"Haebin, honey, when I was young, I was a school teacher for two

years. And I adored everything about my job. Schools socialize and

teach their teachers that you have to behave and fulfill your harmonious obligations to society in a certain way. That as a role model that leads children to college. As a father I could not afford to be a teacher since I had you Haebin when I was too young. Had I been more fortunate to myself I would have waited longer to get married. Haebin, Korea teaches without saying directly. We expect you, children. All of you children in Korea that we have to take care of each other and the poor. When restaurants struggle, it is up to the community to keep sending people to the store to shop there and

make sure he or she succeeds no matter what. Haebin group

harmony in Korea is not a religion, its a lifestyle of hard choices that

mean that if we all spend together carefully. We all know that

restaurant needs the money. Its very easy and important to remember

there are corrupt people everywhere. But how much difference can I

make going by myself as one person who eats a lot versus going as a school where 22 people eat alot and we never

ask for discounts." Said

Her father patiently

"Okay the chicken rotisserie machine literally

cooks chicken one way.

But sometimes the news instructs us, that is all

chicken street food

merchants do certain things. It's not

communism. It's something like it,

``said her father.

Haebin was beginning to cry, thinking her father

was in trouble.

Everyone knows street food merchants are

vagrants she thought. "I

don't get it, I was sitting next to you. We both saw the same news."

"Haebin, this is how South Korea protects us from North Korea.

Instead of saying hey chicken merchant on South Boulevard Seoul, I

want chicken filled with rice porridge and honey. I think its better for

people and its cheaper for you to make. The government has official

news channels for chicken merchants in code. This is how the

government thinks. Why not just tell everyone at the same time, from an Official, Unofficial news channel that always talks about street

rotisserie chicken. And we say okay, we are the government. We have

to instruct the merchants that this is the standard for chicken. Haebin

honey its not funny. It's very serious to get government instructions.

We take our job very seriously to give the kind of food the government

said is good, healthy, nutritious and cheap." Her Father said

"Fine Dad, be weird." Said Haebin

Her Father just said "Honey this is serious. If I do follow the news broadcast advice, I will have a very serious fine. The government last

night instructed all chicken merchants watching that news channel that

rice porridge stuffing has to have almond, jujube, and honey with

brown rice. That is the minimum standard now to sell roasted chicken.

It has to be stuffed and it has to be $9.40 maximum. That is hard, they

understand that is hard. To make money at $9.40 per stuffed chicken.

The local police stations all do it. We are not communist, they will send people to come and buy food. It means we support you and we

as a society are sorry for high prices. All government bureaucrats

think the same. That is why we always have to watch TV. I am a

producer, I am a father, and I will have another restaurant one day. It

is a lot of responsibility to stay in touch with dietary law."

Will It Be The Third Bad Night in Itaewon? By Jason Changkyu Kim,

Purister Publishing and Outsourcing.

Description: This leveled reader talks about Haebin's father's hard life as a genius and the difficulties of starting a drop shipping company in

an uncertain world.

United States English Idioms you will learn:

"Touching Base", "Laying

the Ground Work", "Under Belly", "Drop

Shipping", "Net 15", "Payment

Terms", "Letter of Credit", "Colonialism",

"Colonial Imperialism", "Word

of Mouth"

"Haebin honey in a collectivist society. This is how the news controls

society. Its a different way of Democracy. If there is a news broadcast in Seoul on street chicken in a couple weeks depending on the

urgency of the broadcast: are their food science experts? Are there

cooking shows? Are there national brand advertising. Things like that.

Then you will see if you are careful, the whole country changes over

night. This is the secret information network which is the sad thing

Haebin. The Gangnam raids did not work out because the news talked

for weeks that the iron clamp was coming down." Father said gently and quietly. He gently said "Do you understand?"

"Yes father." Said Haebin,

Haebin quivered a little when she asked "Father what were the

Gangnam district raids about?"

Her father just had a long sigh and a terrible cry.

"Child that is why you

are my daughter. We will never speak of such things in this house.

The raids were supposed to be district wide sweeps in 2010. Maybe

2009. All the news agencies were saying odd ball things about organized crime. There were testimonies, witnesses, and financial reports of what it catastrophically does to the economy. There were a lot of fictional crime shows too about historical reenactments. The news agencies call this buzz. Under the Lee Myung Baek Administration, he was famous for an anti crime program. Buzz in South Korea society always foreshadows crack downs. Everybody knew someone was going to be made an example of but no one suspected it would be the affluent Gangnam

district. That's like 8th

street, nearby Wall Street in New York City. Do

you not remember your

Boston uncle taking us there? No one would

ever expect that such a

wealthy area had such a seedy under belly of

crime." Said her father

"The Crackdown from the police began with

lots of riot police busses

being parked in the area, a lot of cordoned off

sections for anti-police

protests. That's the official start of the police

sweep. I do not know

how many of our brave boys got hurt as detectives." Her father began to get sad again. Then he just kind of tapered off listlessly.

"When the government makes an example of someone or organization my dear Haebin, it gets bad. That's when you have to do public apologies on national television for your failures as a government administrator, television shows demonize your family and investigative reporters blanch your financial connections. And the streets get bad. You have to walk the streets in shame holding a sign

that you are guilty. Korea like the 1960's still very much believes in

"The Street" justice. It's so sad when anything from the dictatorship

era comes back to Korea." Said her father

"Father let's change the subject. Believe it or not, Father I enjoy

talking with you and hearing your opinion." Said Haebin

Haebin continued on saying "I read a book, the Adventures of Park

Min Story 1 and it talked a lot about

dropshipping. The book said and

its a very tiny excerpt. That you have no
inventory, and you sell things
on website. The theory is that you can always
get more stuff from say
The grocery store and the website sells it is as
your own business. Its not
connected to the grocery store. So you buy say
(2) microwaves and sell them on
your website. And you send (1) microwave to
Seoul and (1)
microwave to Incheon City”
“What do you think about that father?” Said
Haebin
Her father just said “Believe it or not, I thought
it was a new idea, there

are 8 trillion people on the planet Haebin. Sooner or later someone has the same idea. I used to do something like drop shipping. At my chicken street restaurant. I bought sandwiches because I did not know how to make them from Itaewon, that's why I know the place is dangerous. I buy 8 or 9 at a time, and I negotiated a discount. Usually and typically it is $3,500 won for a sandwich, each. I buy 8-15 for 500 won each. Which is 50 cents. And I sell it later in the day. Haebin I'm sorry your ashamed he said." Watching her make a face

"Haebin I'm not a chef, I'm a cook. And I'm sorry about that. Haebin

honey, I went to college too. Believe it or not college was around in the

1970's and the internet was not though. I did something like drop

shipping again when you were young Haebin Honey. I had a website.

From a colonialism perspective, teachers teach a big country like the

United States buys 100 Apple Ipods and they sell to South Korea all

100, to one company. That this is a good example of Colonialism and Imperialism. Because they have special contracts with big companies that we call chaebols and that you need a special relationship to sell to chaebols. That way of thinking, that mentality is called 'The Ivy League, Glass Ceiling', the professor reads too many books and says, Hey I know better than you because I am smart. Its easier and more sensible to do drop shipping."

"Dad you have to explain it, you just went on a tangent about drop shipping. I do not understand how drop shipping stops Colonial

Imperialism." Said Haebin Confused

"Ahh... child, you are my doll. I should have explained it more

carefully. Drop shipping is when you do not keep an inventory. You

buy it when you need it. So this is a real website, you can check it my

doll. Any shopping website you can find is a big enough brand, that I can buy from

Certain grocery stores or directly from the site. They support drop shipping

in their own special way. It's about hiring

specialists that can make sure so and so mp3 player from Samsung is

always in stock, that they always have it. It is about two things: these shopping websites

always give me 100 mp3 players when I need it, in the design and model number I want? I said yes they can,

and they did. Can this shopping website in particular, always give it to me in

the price I want? And yes they did. So what does that mean? Haebin

stop being impatient, drop shipping is complicated theory. You will

never find books about it. Someone that knows business like me your father has to teach it to you. So listen. You do this:

A) You call website two thousand zero and contact them in some way. This is

called "Touching Base", its a United States of America Idiom.

You contact them and say hey can I do dropshipping, they say

yes or no and give their contract sales terms

B) You contact the website by writing an email or calling them. And

you "Lay the Groundwork" which is an American idiom that

means something similar to "Touching Base"

C) You negotiate terms, these are small-big companies. I do not
know. You ask 'Net 15' for a letter of credit up to $240. That
means for every chunk of product that you can buy for $240, you
have to pay $240 every 15 days. They are not big retail websites
like the most recognizable brands because I can get a better
product for cheaper from someone else through an simple web search
D) You negotiate to buy a certain amount of product for a certain

price each. And you make a website. Whenever a customer buys

from me, or the company I represent

all the work for me for a small commission. They ship directly to

the customer and I just send them orders

E) This is a way to not do imperialism. Because Colonial

imperialism is the United States. You buy and court a special

relationship with Apple and buy 200 units in United States Dollar.

They buy the

product themselves and ship by (1 or 2 Units at a time). As long as I keep sending them orders, they let me make profit without

having to buy 200 units. That's why they are special "Word of

Mouth Companies" that sell me items only if I send them

customers. Therefore, I am a weird looking contract salesman

with my own store!

Will It be The Fourth Bad Night in Itaewon? By Jason Changkyu Kim

Description: How to make and design a glass cooking table for your

street restaurant. How to make more money per sandwich. And how to design a new street food store!

"Father, how did you make money with a street food store? Sandwiches are only \$2.50 a sandwich?"

"Haebin life was hard and I tried this and that to save money. Propane gas cooking is the most expensive because theres only so many places you can get propane, which is natural gas. I learned hardship, I am giving you family secrets now to save money. You are old enough now. I lost a restaurant after I became a teacher and whatever I learned I saved for street food. I always loved to cook, my daughter.

You have to learn to go to school again. You have to learn how to

make it with very little money. Discipline in staying low with costs and

money is how you become rich. You have to learn science and math

and how to cook with charcoal by measuring heat. Charcoal is the

cheapest cooking method. It's cheaper than electric. Almost." Said Her

Father wisely

"I use Glass Paine 4 inches thick. It has to be 4 inches thick. That is 6 mm wide. You need four cinder blocks. Two on the left and two on the

right. In the middle, under the table you need a container to hold

exactly 3 (2 millimeter pieces of charcoal) that's roughly 4165 degrees

Fahrenheit for 1 hour 18 minutes. Always keep 3 pieces of charcoal lit

in the bucket no more than 3 pieces at a time at 4 inches which is 22

millimeters away from the glass cooking table. Total cost is $122 for

charcoal, cinder block, and thick glass table. It will probably take you

Haebin. And two of your strong cousins 10 minutes to set up and

close. As soon as it cracks you have to get a new glass table pane."

"Of course you have to use cooking oils and grease. Which is

vegetable oil. Meat gets too hot. You should only cook fish"

"Haebin restaurants are all about decorations and interior design.

Sooner rather later you will realize you can get away with more margin

if it looks luxurious. Add $25 to your price if you use glass and

charcoal per fish sandwich. With restaurants,
you need skills to make
money now. You always need more money now
rather than later. You
always need to study math and science Haebin.
It's more important
than English. Without skills you cannot make a
living in life, child."
"Remember if it cracks, you have to get a new
piece of glass. You
clean it like any other cooking surface. Soap and
water is the safest.
Always clean it before you use it." Said her
father, cajoling her to be a

better person. She thought he is always

encouraging me to be a better

person.

Activity 2:

Reading Comprehension Quiz

1. What is the table cookware made out of?

A. Cement

B. Charcoal

C. Glass

2. What is the best product to cook on glass?

A. Cement

B. Meat

C. Fish

3. What is the best cooking method?

A. Gas

B. Gasoline

C. Charcoal

4. What is added margin?

A. Extra profit I can make with different thinking

B. Loss of money (Capital)

C. Lower costs

Answers:

1. C

2. C

3. C

4. A

Will It Be The Fifth Bad Night in Itaewon? By Jason Changkyu Kim

Description: How to Make a stove, the science and mechanics of it,

what Haebin's education taught her on how to fix age old problems.

Literally, The wonders and blessings of women's eduction! Try more

study books! Root Modular Learning Theory, Learning packets by

Jason Changkyu Kim. Purister Publishing and Outsourcing.

"Father, I understand you try hard. And I am sorry that life was hard. I fixed your glass cookware design. Anything that does not melt, crack,

or get too hot is a stove. I use office ash trays. The big ones you see

outside Samsung headquarters. I cut the top off, put it in a nice

container and I filled it with only 3 pieces of charcoal. I was looking at

a Middle Eastern Descent product, called a Hookah, Minah from

Japan, my old friend's cousin was talking about it. At any time we can

make a new stove top. It's not a big deal. Father I have to make it funny, I am sorry about Itaewon, I was just lonely. I almost ruined my life."

"Father I made it funny, I drew this on a piece of scrap paper. The charcoal has to be suspended somehow and it cannot touch the sides. It has to be induction heating. Which is heat the air and tall ash trays are perfect containers that are heat resistant. Father, you used to laugh a lot. I hope this is my way of saying sorry and it helps you with your life." Said Haebin

Reading Comprehension Directions:

Draw where the heat flow goes. Please Identify the subject of the story

and the possessive clauses.

Description and Definitions:

A Subject is the main idea

A Possessive and subjective clause is the supporting Idea

The subject of this graded reader is: Charcoal Cooking in an Ash Tray

The Possessive, Subjective Claus is: Heat Air Flow

Subject -----> A -----> A is Charcoal Cooking in an Ashy Tray

Possessive Clause, Subjective Clause -------> B

-----> B is Heat Air

Flow

Directions:

Please do not be discouraged or ashamed. Please Mark the picture

with A identifying the Subject, Charcoal. And B identifying the

Possessive Clause, Heat Air Flow.

Will It Be The Sixth Bad Night in Itaewon? By

Jason Changkyu Kim

Purister Publishing and Outsourcing

Description: Was Haebin right to run away with father's ideas? We're

see and a diagram to study the supply chain model! How to do profit

and loss and what it means for you!

"Father, I think I made a mistake, this is what textbooks mean by third

party. I bought a consignment of lotion from a store, I know father it

was my life savings. And I bought it with coupons so it was 3 for $5,

and I bought (28) units for $35 of lotion and got 28 bottles. I have been

listing it online at other stores and I got a big order. And I paid my

friends ghost shopping expenses. They are part time employees.

Because you can only use coupons 1 per

customer. But I told the

manager and I am facing a lawsuit for an

unincorporated business and

illegal distribution?" Said Haebin

Her father just sighed.... Haebin is still a child,

she does not

understand anything besides make quick money.

She does not

understand that its really hard to make money.

Was I right? Was I

wrong? I will give my final piece of advice and

we will talk gently,

daughter and father again. If she fails again, I

have to do righteous

father's revenge and stop her from making mistakes again. That's why I am a bad father he thought.

"Haebin, you always have to think about ripple effect. If I drive fast now, what happens to that car next to me tomorrow. Are they going to be scared of Red Hyundai's now?" Said her father gently and carefully to see what he should tell his ambitious Haebin.

"Haebin I will draw you a picture. And you will see its easy and hard to run a business. You need to find a safe 3rd party business that will handle your transactions. If you pay more you pay more for peace of

mind and security. You need to always take credit card because it

gives protection to the consumer. They can cancel and dispute the

purchase or they can always afford to pay you. It's a accounting thing.

Money now when you click buy means money changes hands right

away. Paypal might not be the safest way to pay but it has a function

on it that if you give a tracking number that is 50/50 proof enough that you fulfilled your end of the bargain by shipping it."

"Haebin you need to contact shipping companies carefully, we will do this together or should you have room to do it on your own?"

"It is my business father, I do things on my own." Said Haebin Excitedly

"Then Try this! Try a small company called Stamps.com, United States Postal Service. You have to buy your shipping boxes from United States Cardboard. If you can afford it, you can buy logos for your company. People work hard for their money Haebin, very hard. I worked at fast food places for years for minimum wage, I really admired all these small companies that made it by Halan rules, that pride to your family, pride to your customers, and respect for small profit meant the world to the definition of living a good soulful life!"

Said Her Father

"Shipping per item has to be as follows, its hard to negotiate this. Most opportunities in life are only a series of one chance encounters." Said her Father

"Shipping: Domestic United States, Shoe box size. 5-8 pounds.

$14.99 is normal, it has to be $7.84; they will only allow it if you

guarantee a certain number of shipments. Which is a lot, different

companies and services offer different rates. You need 25 shipments a

month, which is hard. You need to supply a tracking number and

measure the boxes with a weight machine. Priority shipment is too

expensive.

Point Two: Your cost per shipment has to be: the item needs $20

profit, the cost to ship including materials has to be less than $5 per

package. This is the problem with drop shipping, business textbooks

call it ancillary math. You must negotiate this with your drop shipper

otherwise the consignment of 5, 10, 15, 25 units has to be shipped to

you first. Because his shipping rate or her shipping rate is not your shipping rate. So watch papa draw this

diagram for you!" Said Her father with the biggest smile on his face and a black marker holding Haebin's Notebook

5 Box of

Soap (2.99)

Weight:

1 lb

Boxes Weight: 1 lb Total Cost

for Box and

Soap

--------------------> -------------------->

-------------------->

Cost Coupon Cost Coupon Cost Retail

3.25 3 for $5 =

1.06 per 5

pack

$22 for 5 N/A (No

coupon)

5 Box of

Soap + 1

box = 5.56

cost

To make

profit. This

must be

9.41

Profit

Margin

$3. 85 per

5 box of

soap + 1

box

"Okay father, so I made $3.85 per 5 box of soap and 1 shipping box.

But you told me the company does that for me.

You said that right?"

Said Haebin

Her father just thought to himself.... How far do I go with this? "Haebin,

that company is doing you a favor, its kind of weird to sell (1), (5),

even (118) boxes of soap so you can sell it down the street. That

service in dropshipping is free. After everything is said and done.

Unless you handle the products yourself. That you have to courage to make risks and open a real store with your own products. Those

companies will never let you make more than $1-$2 profit per item.

And if you think about it Haebin. All the sales you generate are called

leads. Depending on the contract terms. These leads belong to the

company that drop shipped. Not you Haebin. That's why I stopped

drop shipping. It was a very hurtful experience." Said Her Father, not

sure if I, her father can admit some people were born for business like my Haebin here and some people were born to work. Like me her

father. I am so proud of my daughter sometimes. I guess I will just

keep buying soap from her and hiding it in the house.

Haebin does not know I sent her to old friends thought her father. So I will say yes and no

"Haebin. Drop shipping companies make money three ways. Profit from selling you an item, shipping cost savings, and brand effect.

People know who they are. Honest drop shipper suppliers have too much product inventory. For example. Too much soap so they need to

sell it. That's it. Your contract is what you negotiated. You can change

it anytime. Try to remember they are business partners. Once a month

or once every three months. Ask for a price index? Haebin the world is

dangerous. You have to always protect yourself."

"Okay father, what did you drop ship again?" Said Haebin

"Ummm.... I told you something else and I forgot what I told you.

Uhhhhh... This is my secret. Candy and gum from wholesalers!

Because big boxes are special relationships with manufacturers.

Normal people cannot order them from say Big candy manufacturers.

They always sell okay. You do not need a lot of them. But there are

never coupons." Said her father so knowledgeably.

Will It Be The Seventh Bad Night in Itaewon?

By Jason Changkyu Kim

Purister Publishing and Outsourcing

Haebin's business is starting to take off. She is

not a street food

vendor like her father. But she went back to

Itaewon and made the

mistake of her life. What it means for her small

business?

"Father, I did what you said exactly as you said

it." Said Haebin

"I am having problems with demand and supply.

Supply as the

textbook defines it is how much stuff I can get

all the time. And I went

to Itaewon with my friends and a few of my new friends at the drinking

places said they will be outsourced salesmen. As long as I give them

$4 profit - $24 profit per unit at $100 profit per shipment they will go

door to door for me and I will just supply them with stuff. Which is

candy and gum, and I also have my website which sells candy and

gum.”

“Haebin! No! Oh my gosh, I should have been there for you.” Said her

father ashamed

"You pigeon holed yourself as a small

distributor. Buying small

quantities from the grocery store with coupons.

Now you have too

much demand. When you approached Herhsey's

chocolate or

Cadbury Chocolate, you only had enough

money for something like

one hundred or two hundred boxes. No Haebin!

No! You do not have

a choice, in the modern world you have to buy

one thousand, two

thousand, ten thousand and take the risk now

and figure out your

salesman fleet later. Because the manufacturer has lists, and

protocols and rules. You cannot start at the one hundred or ten box

basket and jump into the one thousand box basket right away or ever.

They will never let you upgrade. In the modern world, you prove

yourself by saying on the second visit, yes I need another one

thousand boxes of chocolate. That's the mistake I made when I

became a street food vendor. You always have to start big and risk it.

That's the hardship of life as a small business owner. When you finally

make it, all the success that you did is what you deserve!" Said her

father.

"Haebin, you must always trust family to do business with you. Do not

trust outsourcing at all. You cannot trust employees you met at a

drinking establishment to sell things earnestly for you. Commission

salesmen are dangerous. You can only trust family to sell a quality

product at a quality price." Said Her Father, demanding her now to be successful

"I had a commission salesmen for Candy, it was between the job I had

as a teacher and before I opened my street food store. I did something

like it and trusted old friends to sell for me. They took advantage of

me. They bought product that I sold: candy and gum, that I was

importing from dropshipping from other countries and my secret list of

import stores and they used me to supply them with a lot for a very

cheap price while they faked the sales chart. I thought business was really booming and when I ran out of money, I had a bad name

everywhere. People said I was re-selling stuff from other stores which

I never intended Haebin. I did to get ideas on what to sell which is the

worst I ever did to people Haebin. I found out that all these import

stores will not let me shop there anymore. And the import companies I

was dealing with like all things would not sell to me anymore. Because

my friends stole my business. They were buying at artificially cheap

prices. I sold them candy and gum at $4 profit
per unit, they just
stockpiled the products and used me to source
products for them. This
deeply hurt me for years because I wanted a
business that I could
pass to you Haebin and I wanted my friends to
be a part of that too.
After two years of okay profit, I called it quits,
my friends are now
some of the biggest candy distributors of
imported candy in South
Korea now. It hurt so much when my old friends
left me like that." Said
her father so sadly.

Will It Be the Eighth Bad Night in Itaewon? by Jason Changkyu Kim.

Purister Publishing and Outsourcing

Haebin Did It. She did amazing things in her life but she could not let

go of how her father ruined her life. And 'Tis the sadness of our ages,

that she let her fathers dreams go for her own. Read the final chapter

of the Haebin, Itaewon Series.

"Father I learned in economic class. Mom said I was not ready to go to

college. I goto hagwon to learn principles of business. I have my own business now father I don't need college. Evergreen is far and lonely"

"Oh my dear Haebin. You don't want to go? I have heartbreak now child" Said her Father

"Please tell your father why you don't want to go"

"It's because I don't have to go. I learn economics everyday at hagwon. Why should I go to college if I am successful on my own?" Haebin said

"Child please. I'm begging you this. This is small money. You have to go to college. That's why life didn't work out for me and it did when

you were born. Please child your father went to college. My daughter

will go to college." Her father pleaded

"Father no why should I study. I have 11,000 dollars now and two

employees. Why should I wait? Life is passing me by" Argued Haebin

"Harbin business cannot wait. After college you won't be able to do it

again. The moment passed you by because you chose to do

something different and better. Please 11,000 is small money. You

can't buy a house,you can barely afford a car"
Chided her father

"Harbin you are going to college so you don't
have to make your

mothers choice and just become a housewife.
Do you understand

Haebin. You will be a CEO one day." Said her
father oblivious that he

was losing the argument

"I'm already a CEO. I have 11,000 dollars.
Father please listen to me

you don't understand how successful I am. I
have gross sales of 1.2

million won a month. That's 1200 dollars." Said
Haebin

"Daddy thats big money. I am a successful person now!" Said Haebin

"Haebin, having a life. A Family is 7,200 dollars a month. You do not know what you are talking about. Just like Itaewon, I told you to stop hanging around that bad neighborhood. This is small change money, 1200 dollars a month is nothing." Said Her Father

"Then this conversation is over" Said Haebin

"Haebin Please, please listen to your father." argued her father

"No dad, you listen to me, this conversation is over. That nice solider left ages ago. Mother said I am not ready to study abroad and I have a

business now. This conversation is over!" Yelled Haebin

"Please Haebin, listen to me, I will take over your business and you

will go back to college in Korea." Said her father authoritatively

"No, I am not running away from home, I am just not going to college

anymore. Forget that bother!" Said Haebin and with that the

conversation was over….. Haebin dropped out of college and ruined her life. Within a few months she married one of her coworkers and

had a small family. Her father cried in sorrow for years, knowing the

the impetus Haebin ruined her life because he said no years ago in

the wrong way. Telling her how to have a business before she was

ready...

What's the Matter with Itaewon? The Epilogue.
By Jason Changkyu Kim
Purister Publishing and Outsourcing. December 18 2022.

Foreword: Jason Changkyu Kim continues the Will It Be an Bad Night In Itaewon Series with the Sequel, Part Two. Lamenting the joys and failures of being an father. Haebin's father understands sorrow, tragedy, and it is reminiscent of fortitude in trials of tibulation. It makes sense that things happen and as the snow ball gets larger and larger. You understand more and you are finalized in your heart that everything will be okay!

It has been an long time since Haebin finally grew up and got her own business? 'Tis an sadness that her life ended earlier than most. Because she had an family before she could understand or comprehend the fullness of her decision to date early. But, alas what will happen to Haebin's father or her sweet mother? The breadwinners of the family that made sure all the bills were paid and done in earnest. Let us delve deeper into the pie of Haebin's breadwinners.

Haebin's father was on the sidewalk weeping in sorrow. He was reminiscing of his days as an barista at an small cafe. Thinking… I do not think like that anymore. That I did that, I discovered so and so. Haebin's father had the deepest heartbreak. Dropshipping was for my daughter to be happy not to settle and say okay women are not meant to own businesses. I was thinking back a long time ago when Haebin was pregnant and I was an Barista at an cafe. I discovered that method and they made so much money. I hope they keep me in mind when I tell them my sorrows and experience.

For an small cafe, the barista is the expresso machine attendant. We had an only an Jinsung JS 1 BW Water Heater and an Cafe Madenee Expresso Bar Maker. We had purchased it from Gmarket South Korea. And I told them, its hard to make an new word. What it means, what it feels like. American Coffee is drip coffee. Let us call this an Americano and I will make one expresso and add two cups of purified water. And now it has the same strength but stronger flavor of an drip American Coffee.

"Manager we are an small company, we have to save money where ever we can. Please? For the continued blessings of this business. My daughter is pregnant with child and I need to make ends meet until things work out for our drop shipping business."

And he went on an tangent explaining his great idea. An drop shipping business. And the manager just took advantage of him and took all these great ideas and put them in his own companies. And the manager thought to herself, all I need is an token of my appreciation.

Haebin's father will receive 4,000,000 Won and I will terminate his employment. No more, no less child. You should have learned to talk less openly about your anguish and problems.

Haebin's father thought "When I was younger, I enjoyed shoe shopping with my mother and father. South Korea started fabricating shoes an little late. Probably in the 1970s to 1980s. My daughter bought me Excelsior Brand, Industrial Classics. Which is part of the 2022 Collection. Until 1984 or 1985 those little odds and ends that people rely on everyday were imported. Difficult things like shoes, jacket linings, belt buckles. All had to be imported, I guess Haebin know. I feel bad, something changes in my face when I have to purchase imports. It is just hard even in South Korea. Only one or two things is manufactured by Korea. As part of my everyday wardrobe. It is fortunate that we work hard as an people that used car auto mobile exports worked out. That we can afford as an nation, to import things. But in everyday reality we have to settle and that is the hardship of just running things. That is what Chairman Bacchus and the Peoples Power Party of Korea means to elderly Koreans. Does the country have it? The country needs it. The country can afford resale to the country's inhabitants. Very slowly, we in South Korea will fabricate our own brands and quantity types of products such as Excelsior Shoes."

Haebin's Father was sitting at an cafe. At an Convenience store. Thinking back to moments with Haebin. "Haebin child, do you remember South Korean Jin Ramen, it debuted in the 1990s. It was your favorite. I loved making new snacks for you. Try this one when you are happy at home playing by yourself. South Korean Jin Ramen Blue. Korean Sesame Seed Oil, Honey, and Coffee Creamer. Drain out the ramen broth, and mix together with the noodles. Add Japanese or Sempo Korean Soy Sauce and eat your noodles. Its an sweet snack that we can enjoy together."

Haebin's father was contemplating Drop shipping again as an model of growth for Haebin. "My gosh, Haebin likes clothes though, is it wise to sell clothes? She would probably keep it all for herself." Haebin's father began to groan… whimper.. and with one deft finger wiped his nose. There are several Korean Brands that are a little more infamous than others. Haebin's father thought. There is only an few brands for women's wrist watches from South Korea and And South Korean style

Women's Jackets, Overcoats, and Women's Sweaters.

"It makes sense in an fashionable world." He thought. Men he mused, think about function. Function is not it is cute to dress nice and look sweet. Men's fashion tends to be layers. An sweater, an Collared Shirt, an overcoat jacket, and some long underwear. Is an great option for myself as an father. As I get older I realized sadly, you do have to look good. I would probably be an dark blue almost navy, and dark tan beige color schemed person. By layering up, at any time I could stop by my motor vehicle car and drop off extra layers. It is important to be presentable in an shallow world. Snowboarding in modern times, is about layered warmth. Long sleeved T Shirts, Thermal Vests, Then an Jacket, and an Overcoat. It helps too when you fall to be warm and soft. That is what I would propose in an sales model, always try to make the basket bigger and more wholesome. You only go shopping once in a while, not so much everyday. It has to be cheap, in American I remember my Boston Brother said about 600 dollars for an outfit. That's the thing brother, the issue is, how often do you buy and in what quantity? It has to be fashionable. I tend to stay in Tommy Hilfiger Nauticus, I am wealthy but cheap. I look cheap, thus I do not have safety concerns in New York

City where crime is famously high but, I do want to look nice for Haebin's mother, so it is back to Navy or Dark Beige.

"What would I say Haebin" Her father thought quietly.

"When I was young, before you were born." Her father mused to himself. "I was an salesman, today's generation no longer believes in it. Sales is how you grow an brand. You cannot just build an website or storefront branch. You need to advertise very carefully and prudently and build your reputation. This is the normal process of everyday life. An client book is very valuable to any business. And these one, one, one, two, one sales encounters are very important. I cannot go through that hardship of life again. Enticing people to stop by the restaurant and favor me with patronage. You must learn to hire, train, and retain, and acquire talented sales teams. If you are wrong. You go to mental hospitals or jails if you are reckless with your sales teams. Sales teams are stage one advertising. Advertising teams are stage two sales. You cannot have one without the other. An sales team can create value in something that people do not value at all. For example, used car automobiles. An used automobile is worthless to people interested in cars. An good mechanic can fix it up until its refurbished okay. And hopefully our client will remember our skills and services? And start their own taxi or freight forwarding fleet."

"The key to an good city car motor vehicle is frequent braking and frequent acceleration. Turning radius is not so important but important enough you need an sub compact like an KIA Ray or an KIA Soul. It has an rear view camera on it for parallel parking. The automobile car parts you can buy or obtain from an good shopping website in South Korea very good spark plugs Korean origin or Japanese Densha Origin. Very good for the price and quantity of your fleet. Haebin, I used to previously work for an small parcel delivery firm. The owner, an old wizened man started selling fried chicken and he was not keen on using auto bicycles to deliver food. He thought it was foolish and an unnecessary hardship. He used an KIA Ray and it was 2004 model that was quite nimble and clever for frequent braking. The KIA Ray has an 1.0 gasoline engine and it had good gasoline mileage, about 28 miles per gallon. An very clever mechanic and ahh… Haebin my gosh! Your father is bragging again. No no no shhh….! The motor vehicle was very easy to take care of. I purchased it for him, I recommended the purchasing of this vehicle from Auto Wini South Korea and he adored the vehicle. An chance to be warm and prudent during Korea's cold winters." Haebin's father thought cheerfully

Haebin's father thought "That owner, the fried chicken owner did not use me or take advantage of me as much as most. But, it was still hard to work for an greedy owner. I had hoped we could become friends, I needed to work and he had an opportunity available to me. To make fried chicken, it is my own recipe I told him. You need chicken wings and legs. And no eggs, you can use egg whites if you dare but, you do not need the yolks. The orange part inside the egg. You need Ottogi flour from South Korea or Panko Bread Crumbs from Japan, you need to mix it gingerly with salt and pepper and mix it very gently but thoroughly into an sludge and wash the chicken wings and legs with water. Then you put this sludge syrup with an little Korean grape seed cooking oil mixed with the sludge and gently and carefully pile the sludge onto the chicken wings and chicken legs. When it is ready you boil them in more grape seed cooking oil or brown rice cooking oil from Korea and take it out of the boiling cooking oil when it is nice and brown. Very crispy. American Vegetable Oil makes sense but the quality and quantity of your cooking oil decides the flavor of your fried chicken skin. Is it salty and savory like I would prefer you to enjoy

Haebin? Then you must use Korean Grape Seed Cooking oil or Korean Brown Rice Cooking oil. If you are not sure what to do, you must always thicken the batter with more Ottogi Korean Flour. It is an mixture of rice flour and white wheat flour"

Gheez… my gosh.. It feels like I let Haebin always walk all over me. Haebin's father was thinking to himself "What wast that guy's name, Joshua or David or Thomas? I wish I had to courage to talk to Haebin more firmly. You cannot marry United States Army, do you understand? It is not an good job, is he planning to live in Korea with us? Will he move his mother and father to Korea to live with us? I am glad you married your coworker from the drop shipping company. It is important that you live in Korea with your mother and father Haebin? What are you going to do if Joshua convinced you to move to Missouri. Haebin, I am your father. I do everything for you, I cook, I clean, I even taught you how to run an business. Did Joshua the combat captain know how to do any of these complicated things? His issue was well… I do not have to. No Joshua it is not okay that you finished college already and you are dating my daughter who is still in university and you keep telling her you can support our family and I have to give you allowance money all the time. Joshua just use the money exchange at any

South Korean Bank, you do not need to spend United States dollars here to impress Haebin's family. I never understood why you could not get married in America to an nice American girl. You do not need Haebin right?"

Today was an difficult morning. Haebin's father thought to himself. "I was thinking about Haebin again." he thought. I do it. The grand it. When I think about my wife and how things worked out with Haebin. My wife just started blaming me one day. Haebin's mother. About Joshua and about Haebin not finishing university. I have been pondering and thinking and acting more lately. Lashing out to ghosts in my closet and memories in my mirror on my desk. I have not done 'That' for an very long time. In the deepest pits of sorrow and sadness. I do 'that'. I collect my porcelain toys my grandmother gave me and I play with them on my desk. How poor our family was Haebin. How sad and tired I am now. All my awards are on the wall above my desk. What promising future and success meant to me. An lonely room. An lonely soul. And never an good answer for anything. In that sense of the word 'The' means, solace and answers. After an certain amount of time Haebin. 'The' means more of the same. More hardship and no clear explanation why it is so gosh darn it important to bother me all the time with life's trivial problems or promises of problems. Joshua should have known better not to date an young girl still present in active university. It is not okay that I had to hide my feelings for years Haebin. Because you would not listen to your father. Haebin, I adore you every present moment of every continuous day. Why could you not listen to me and just stay single?. Every time I go out, I only buy an small cup of coffee for myself. And I always buy whatever snack you loved the most to brighten your day. The waffle store is far away from our house or where I and your mother lived. Almost 32 minutes in the wrong direction. Haebin in my heart I do not know who will take care of you if

I pass from sickness, stress, or old elderly age. Every day I am buying you your favorite foods and drinks. I like to! I like that very much. Why can you not listen to me more gently when I am stern. Perhaps an little to firm today? Haebin you cannot date until you are ready to settle down. Please think about the boy, this nice Korean boy saved his whole life so we can have an apartment and motor vehicle car early. It is very important to find, date, and capture an good spouse. Life time mate for the soulful completion of life!

"Haebin… When you were at that girls high school. I in my heart was happy. Blessed that Korea is great. Blessed that Korea cared so much, it is an all girls high school, public school. Private school uniforms. How blessed we are that Korea tried so earnest! So devoutly hard! I wanted everything to be perfect for Korea. All the time!" He thought with tears forming in his eyes. "When Korea did high quality public school, I fell in love. This is home! Forever more! And I felt the deepest anguish when the teachers at your high school. I felt in the pit of my soul were just going through the motions. I was an believer. How much Korea cares about education. And it hurt so much when I found an loophole. Probably like how that young boy teacher, felt about the Genealogical Family Tree. That the parents can with permission of the Korean Justice Department, allow their children to use their identification numbers and work at an job in South Korea while they get their own residency visas. That the epistemology of the word family tree, means house from within. If your job is okay with it, then use your parents identification number and you will be sure to get your own visa? And it hurt because, that weird gentleman and old lady just kept saying that young boy will quit soon. If the law allows it, then it is not an big deal that I take it an step further. It is my job now that all the hard work is done and I will continue using his identification residency visa. If he is not here, then he is not here. My friends will ruin him in America too! How badly he makes me look. This restaurant is so important to my family. Italian luxury food. No white wheat pasta, same genuine taste. And I thought, I guess….. it is important but not so singularly important it evolves into an nuclear bomb on an ant?" And Haebin's Father listened gently to Daniel Jang's Violin Piece, 'The River Flows in you' and thought on the T hymn…. I lost the school, I had an foreboding feeling that if the teachers do not believe in their careers and their place of employment like I adored them as an high school parent. That in my soul and heart, it is terrible thing and malady to see, I give up in an teacher. How much effort used to previously go to making an wonderful day of lessons and articles. Replaced with 'One more week… One more week… Arghh! I passed my performance review! Do not have to try again hard until next year!" And Haebin's father thought, that young boy teacher has no idea what he did to me, How much anguish I felt that he let go. It is not okay, these are people, they are not cattle. And that fine young boy became an terribly corrupt man as the years rolled by. Fallen from grace is so harsh and sad.

I thought to myself "When did that young boy teacher leave?" And he had the saddest reason he said "Two fold reasons. My grandmother said it is an reason that makes sense to an really old lady that remembers 1954 California and you are not happy with the spiritual failure of this girls high school. You feel the sting and bitterness that they do not care to an fault. Your personality is 'Hard headed'." And that young boy teacher said the strangest thing that clicked to me Haebin, your father. That he understands and does not understand the severe repercussions of what happened. At the young age of 24 he would say 'It is an kind of xenophobia or racism that there is no word for yet even if I am biological Korean like the students are.' absentmindedly thought Haebin's father. "No I understand it, his Korean is okay and not bad. It is an kind of..... whish wash push and pull that is too orchestrated for the students age group. It is like the kind of manipulation you would get from an trillion dollar oil deal with security teams and wiretapping and negotiations. It makes sense he is special because he is an high school teacher at 22 but it makes sense it is so dreadfully serious and scientifically technological that too many important people are here. Period. Period. Do not question you have to run away now! And Haebin's father said "Yes!".... "See? Haebin" he turned to look at an invisible ghost of his daughter. "This is the problem with young people. That is how he acts. He does not appreciate the gravity and seriousness of the situation. If you see an landmine. You do not stand still and samurai crouch with an sword and say…………. Hum…………. Yes!" "And just stand there and look confused to be cool to nobody!"

"Hard Headed!" "There is no more greater meaning to Hard Headed!" Wizened Haebin's very old father.

That young boy teacher. My gosh………

"Thinks too much!" Yes…. He nodded and thought… Yes! He thinks too much.